THE SODBUSTER'S WIT AND WISDOM

Poems by
Danny Smith

Illustrations by
Deborah Smith Hall
and
James L. Johnson

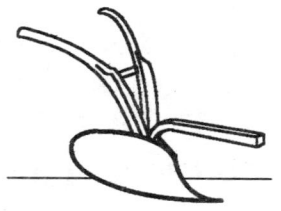

    The Sodbuster Poet has compiled his thoughts into another collection of poems containing his wit and wisdom about farm life and human nature. Danny acknowledges the importance of including faith in God in all aspects of life.

    Join The Sodbuster Poet as he relates some humorous experiences as a farmer and some serious thoughts about people and life.

Copyright, ©, 1997
Danny L. Smith
All rights reserved.

No part of this publication may be reproduced or transmitted in any form or by any means, electronic or mechanical, including photocopy, recording, or any information storage and retrieval system, without permission in writing from the publisher.

Requests for permission to make copies of any part of this work should be mailed to:

Sodbuster Poet
Danny L. Smith
1754 W. 130th Ave. N.
Milton, Kansas 67106
(316)478-2496
sodbusterpoet@Juno.com

ISBN: 0-9652605-1-8

Printed in the USA by

MORRIS PUBLISHING

3212 East Highway 30 • Kearney, NE 68847 • 1-800-650-7888

CONTENTS

THE SODBUSTER'S WIT

Bountiful Harvest 3
Machinery 6
Coffee Shop Justice 9
Why I'm a Farmer
    (or Why I'm Not a Cowboy) 12
A Cowboy's Strength
    by Melanie Smith 15
Intellectual Producers 17
Family Farm 21
Custom Cutters 24
The Harvest of '97 27
The Old Hayrack 33
Meditation 37
Outdoor Comfort 38
Farm Wives 41
I Forgot 44
The Cruise 47
Teddy 54

THE SODBUSTER'S WISDOM

Life's Walk 56
A Changed Man 59
Timeless Words 62
My Son 65
The Season 66
Success 68

DEDICATION

Most of us don't have a choice as to where we are born or how we are raised. The good Lord blessed me by allowing me to be born in America and raised on a farm by Christian parents.

I would like to dedicate this book to the memory of my parents, Arthur and Rachel Smith.

A special thanks to my wife, Karen, for being editor and publicist. Also thanks to Debbie Hall and James L. Johnson for the great art work.

Thanks to my daughter, Melanie, for her support and contribution to my book.

THE

SODBUSTER'S

WIT

This poem was published in my first book and seemed to be a favorite so I've included it in this book.

Harvest time can get pretty hectic and I always get in a hurry. That leaves room for error and something usually gets forgotten.

BOUNTIFUL HARVEST

T'was the night before harvest,
I couldn't sleep like I should.
I was thinkin' about wheat
And it sure did look good.

I bet it'll make forty,
And, if the storms don't move in,
By this time tomorrow
We'll have wheat in the bin.

The combine and trucks
Were all parked in a row.
If the wind blows by ten,
We'll be ready to go.

I gave up at five
And sprang from the bed.
I opened the door
And looked out toward the shed.

The combine was there;
The breeze was a-blowin'.
The sky was all clear;
Looks like we'll be goin'.

I threw on my clothes
And ate in a flash.
Then out to the outhouse
I made a quick dash.

Back to the garage
To feed the dogs and the cats,
I grabbed four cans of bug spray
To keep off the gnats.

I ran to that combine
Like I had one day to live.
Checked the sickle and cylinder
And reset the sieve.

I tightened the chains
Till they were all just so-so.
My watch read ten o'clock;
I was ready to go.

I drove to the field
And threw her in gear.
The sound of that combine
Was all I could hear.

I cut clear through the quarter
And was half back again,
When I thought I would check
To see what's in the bin.

What in the heck!
Did my eyes deceive me?
The bin was clean empty,
No wheat did I see.

In all of the hurry
And fury and hopin',
I guess I'd forgot
And left the cleanout door open.

After the shoutin' and gesturin'
And the air became clear,
I said, "Well, the pheasants
Will eat good this year."

A little spilled grain
Can't do any harm,
When the Lord has allowed me
To work on this farm.

You know the rest of that harvest
Went as smooth as could be.
We had a good crop;
I think it made forty-three.

And every harvest since then,
About one day before,
I make a special point to check
That bin cleanout door.

It seems something is always breaking down on the farm and it's hard to find parts. I've said and heard it said many times, I wonder what engineer designed that thing. Read this poem and you'll know.

MACHINERY

Farm machinery can be nice,
But it'd be easier to bear it.
If the engineers that design the stuff
Had to come out and repair it.

Those knucklebustin' places
That a guy can hardly reach,
Confusion and complexity
Is what the colleges must teach.

Nuts and bolts of every size,
Both metric and U.S.A.
Special wrenches by the score
Adds to the price you have to pay.

Those engineers must laugh and joke
When they find the right design,
That has you standin' on your head
Lookin' back at your behind.

They put grease zerks where you can't grease,
And tighteners that do not tighten.
Chains and sprockets of every sort
Leave you cussin' and a fightin'.

Bearings by the millions,
No two are the same.
The parts place always has them all,
Except the one you name.

That model's discontinued;
They don't make that any more.
Do you still have one of those?
That was obsolete in '84!

Tractors, combines, discs and drills,
Enough parts to fill the sea.
No wonder parts men are always mad
And take it out on me.

Combines are a nightmare.
You fight 'em tooth and nail.
After a week or so of harvest,
You're wishin' it would hail.

I told the wife
Nothin' could make me meaner,
Than to have to harvest the rest of my life
With my 1981 Gleaner.

If the Lord let's me in heaven,
I just ask one small prayer.
That I run that combine for eternity
And not have one repair!

Any place there's a small town cafe or coffee pot farmers usually gather to discuss yields. Every community seems to have one ol' boy who always has better wheat, better cattle, or whatever. This poem's for him.

COFFEE SHOP JUSTICE

We were gathered at the coffee shop
Just before dawn,
One pot was drank
And another one put on.

They kept driftin' in
Till the tables were full,
We were eatin' and drinkin'
And shootin' the bull.

I knew what would happen,
There'd be no mistake,
My neighbor would ask,
"What'd your wheat make?"

It seems every harvest
For twenty years or more,
He just happens to beat me
By three bushels or four.

So I thought just for spite
And to give me some pleasure,
I'd add four or five bushel
Just for good measure.

I'd poured my third cup
When I heard from the rear,
"Well, Danny boy,
What'd your wheat make this year?"

I said, "You know,
I'd have to confess,
It was a real good crop,
About forty-five, I guess."

He didn't even notice
Who'd just walked in late,
He just blurted out,
"Mine made forty-eight!"

Well, his landlord was sittin'
About two chairs down.
He raised up his head
And he turned clear around.

He said, "You know,
Just to be fair,
Call down to the Co-op
And transfer my share."

"When I figured my part,
As I always do,
It only came out
To about forty-two."

Well, that old boy's face
Turned as red as a beet,
And he stomped out the door
In total defeat.

Except for the day
That I married my wife,
That had to be the
Best day of my life.

It was almost two months
Before he wandered back in,
But every time I think of it,
I get a big grin.

So before you go braggin'
Over coffee shop chat,
Be darn sure you know
Where your landlord is at.

People often ask why I'm not a cowboy poet, so I wrote this poem as an explanation. We never had horses on our farm and we mainly chase cattle around with three wheelers and pickups. The cowboy poets do a great job of writing about ranching, so I thought I would tell the farmer side.

WHY I'M A FARMER
OR
WHY I'M NOT A COWBOY

When the Lord led me to farmin',
I guess He chose the right course.
I wouldn't have made a cowboy.
I just don't like a horse.

I'd much rather sit
In my John Deere every day,
Than bounce on a horse
And feed the thing oats and hay.

They're big; they smell;
They bite and they kick.
They're either spookin' the cattle
Or gettin' cut up or sick.

When you need to use one
And try to go fetch it,
It runs off to the pasture
And you never can catch it.

They'll make you so mad,
You want to haul off and hit 'em.
But besides all those things,
My body don't fit 'em.

My legs are too short
To reach the stirrups with my feet.
And the saddle's too wide.
My cheeks don't fit the seat.

Cowboy hats won't stay on.
I have no use for chaps.
I wear lace up work boots
And free seed company caps.

I once went with a Colorado friend
On a day long trail ride.
That little rivet on the seat of my jeans
Rubbed off all the hide.

When we got back to the ranch,
I wanted out of the saddle.
But we spent 2 more hours with the neighbor
Helpin' him sort cattle.

My legs were so sore I couldn't walk.
My butt looked like beef steak.
I knew if God would let me live,
It's the last trail ride I'd take.

When it comes to ridin',
I'll take my own advice.
It may be cool to cowboy,
But pickups ride twice as nice.

When I get the urge to work cattle,
I'll call my ol' blue heeler,
Get a bale of hay and a bucket of grain
And run 'em in with my four wheeler.

My daughter, Melanie, is a song writer at heart, but I liked her poem about cowboys, so I've included it. I think it would make a good song, too.

A Cowboy's Strength
by Melanie Smith

It's a tough row to hoe when your goin' against the grain,
When your buckin' the system and cussin' the rain.
It comes from a strength buried deep down inside,
That festers and boils 'til it can no longer hide.

It'll push you to glory and drive you to pain,
But it never gives up; it always remains.
Who possess this strength to keep drivin' on?
And never gives up 'til the last hope is gone?

It's the one with the hat brim turned up in a grin.
It's the one with the jeans that the saddle's worn thin.
It's the hard working hero we'd all like to claim.
Some may call him boring or stupid or plain,
But we all know better 'cause Cowboy's his name.

Most people have heard the term "dumb farmers". Too often we're portrayed that way on T.V. and in the movies. I resent that and so I wrote this poem for those folks that think their food is grown in the grocery store and doesn't come from the farm.

INTELLECTUAL PRODUCERS

Some call us dumb farmers.
They imply we have no brains.
They think we simply plant the seed
And pray to God it rains.

There's no need to worry
About those input costs.
If we have a failure,
Uncle Sam makes up what's lost.

No old machinery to repair
Or implements to buy.
Just tell the banker what you want
And it falls out of the sky.

No need to get excited
And work fifteen hour days.
There's no livestock to tend
Or kids we have to raise.

The wife, she doesn't need to work
Or soil her curly locks.
She just walks out and pulls that check
From the U.S. mail box.

Maybe we should give those folks
A course in higher learning.
Let 'em pitch manure all day
And see how much *they're* earning.

Average farmers get bad press,
While the big ones get the money.
But to suggest that we're all stupid
Really isn't very funny.

We're soil stewards and mechanics,
Cowboys and business men.
We work hard to raise our families
And get the crops put in.

We provide our country meat and bread
And feed many overseas.
If American farmers were forced to quit,
It'd bring nations to their knees.

So before you call us stupid
And names I won't repeat.
Just thank the Lord at supper time
We produce the food you eat.

The average age of a farmer today is between 58 and 60 years old. That means not many young people are coming back to the farm and that concerns me a great deal. I wonder what will happen to our farmland. I hope corporate farming does not get to be the normal way.

The poem <u>Family Farm</u> is about a grandpa watching his grandson play and wondering if he will get the chance to operate the family farm.

FAMILY FARM

The old man stood and shook his head.
He'd never seen the like.
His grandson was growin' up,
There ridin' on his trike.

I wonder what his future holds,
Will he get to farm someday?
Or will family farms become extinct
And go the corporate way?

Will he have the chance I've had
To be steward of the soil?
Will he experience the fruits of sweat
And long, hard years of toil?

Lord, I know I've been blessed
To live upon this land,
And watch the ways of nature
That are guided by Your hand.

Those sunrises that stir the soul,
The smell of new mown hay,
The miracle of a newborn calf,
On a snowy winter's day.

Fawns that play at field's edge,
Pheasants in the spring,
The colors of the wildflowers
That timely rains can bring.

Golden waves of grain
From fields the plow will till.
Droughts and storms that take the crops
And test a farmer's will.

This farm's been good to me,
Though I haven't made a lot.
My needs were always met;
I'm happy with what I've got.

Four generations have farmed this land,
That boy would make it five.
I guess that'd be a dream come true,
If it'd happen while I'm alive.

So, Lord, I'd like to ask
For something in advance.
If that young boy would like to farm,
I pray he'll have the chance.

CUSTOM CUTTERS

They arrived late one afternoon,
The unloading had begun.
Let's get those headers on tonight
While we still have some sun.

Park the campers; cook the food;
Supper would be late.
Five hundred acres of golden grain
Lay in the field in wait.

Supper over and time for bed,
The evening's jobs all done.
We've got a lot to do tomorrow;
We'll be up with the sun.

Up and dressed and breakfast ate,
The boss could feel the strain.
The sky was clear this morning,
But the forecast called for rain.

The combines all checked and fueled;
The crew was set to go.
The farmer gave directions,
Down the road two miles or so.

The ground was dry; the wheat was good;
The grain rolled in the bin.
If the rain holds off till nine tonight,
We'll get this crop put in.

Late afternoon the pace picked up;
Storm clouds began to build.
The field would make sixty,
If one more truck was filled.

The last swath just filled the truck
And he headed on to town.
As dark skies opened up
And rain came pouring down.

The farmer arrived with waving arms
As they told him of the yield,
But he broke down and cried,
"You crazy fools, you cut the neighbor's
    field!"

The wheat in south central Kansas looked real good going into spring this year (1997), but on April 11th we had a real hard freeze and everyone thought the crop was gone. We were all depressed for sometime. But the crop went ahead and developed. In fact, we had a record crop. This poem is about that experience and the trials and tribulations of harvest. May the Lord bless your crop.

THE HARVEST OF '97

I've seen strange things
That the weather brings,
But one I won't forget.

Was on April 11
of '97.
No one's explained it yet.

Arctic air blew in
On a stiff north wind.
The mercury began to drop.

And I knew darn well
That a bad cold spell
Could mean a failed wheat crop.

To check how low
The temperature would go,
A thermometer was placed near ground.

At six that night
I got a fright.
Twenty-eight was what I found.

When the sun did rise
On cold clear skies,
I didn't want to look.

And I wore a frown
As I bent way down.
My cold, bare hand it shook.

Twenty degrees it read.
It was surely dead.
The stems were froze clear through.

As I walked away
In great dismay,
I said, "What will we do?"

It was a somber stop
At the coffee shop.
The heads were all hung low.

The agronomist's reports
Had us out of sorts.
It'd be harvest before we'd know.

My cousin, Lyle,
He didn't smile.
He checked his plants each day.

A miracle we'd need
To get our seed.
All we could do was pray.

And we were blessed.
The crop progressed.
The spring was cool and wet.

The plants they healed
And the split stems sealed.
We might have a wheat crop yet.

Everyone was thrilled
When the wheat had filled.
The heads were full of grain.

As harvest neared,
The thing we feared
Was too much hail and rain.

So we kept our eyes
On the western skies,
And the fields turned golden brown.

On the 19th of June,
In a harvest moon,
I cut my first full round.

I was amazed at the yield
I got from that field.
I called my cutters real fast.

I need it done,
While we have the sun.
This weather may not last.

They arrived next day.
We were cuttin' away
When in my landlord wheeled.

I was cuttin' on me
And he could see
His wheat still in the field.

I unloaded the bin,
Folded the auger in.
I'd get away with any luck.

But I lost my mind.
I didn't look behind
And I backed into the truck.

The unloading auger crinkled.
The straw chopped wrinkled.
The truck side caved in.

My face turned green
When I saw the machine
And all that smashed up tin.

I know I said
Some words I'd dread
As we tore the thing apart.

I got parts next day,
Put 'em on right away,
And by two we were ready to start.

Things were going my way.
We'd be done in one day.
The bins were almost filled.

One more landlord to go
And wouldn't you know,
Storm clouds began to build.

It rained all right.
An inch that night.
The fields were pretty wet.

We'd need some sun
To get it done.
All we could do was set.

The next day we'd test,
But it wasn't the best.
We mainly just got stuck.

It'd take a day or so
Before we could go.
Then we'd need some luck.

It rained once more.
I knew the score.
My cutters would leave for home.

And I guess I knew
The old M2
Would finish it all alone.

The fields got dry
The eighth of July.
The crop was finally in.

I doubt I'll see
Another sixty-three,
Come my way again.

I've seen strange things
That the weather brings,
But a miracle come from heaven.

And a record to top
From a frozen wheat crop
In nineteen ninety-seven.

A friend inspired me to write this poem by calling to my attention how many uses the hayrack has had and how many people it has carried.

THE OLD HAYRACK
inspired by thoughts from Jay Gosch

It's been around the farm, I guess,
Long before I was born.
My dad used it for bundle feed
And haulin' home shucked corn.

I remember feedin' cows
When I was just a kid.
The bales we hauled on it
Was the least of what it did.

It has carried many a man
And many a bale to stack.
At the end of the day when all was done,
Many a darn sore back.

It went on numerous hayrack rides.
Held pumpkins on Halloween.
Carried floats at town parades
And many a homecoming queen.

It helped build a young boy strong
Loadin' alfalfa hay,
And served as stage on Saturday night
For the band that came to play.

It's been to neighbor's auctions,
A garage sale here and there.
Held nativity scenes at Christmas
And hauled carolers everywhere.

The farms are fewer now,
More efficient, so they say.
No need to own the three or four
It took to put up hay.

The big round bale retired it.
It's planks are not so strong.
But it's had a very useful life;
One that's good and long.

It's not used much nowadays.
It sits alone outback.
But I see a thousand memories
Piled on that old hayrack.

Not many people today get to experience the joy of an outhouse.
I still have one on my farm and find it peaceful and relaxing, except for an occasional hazard or two.

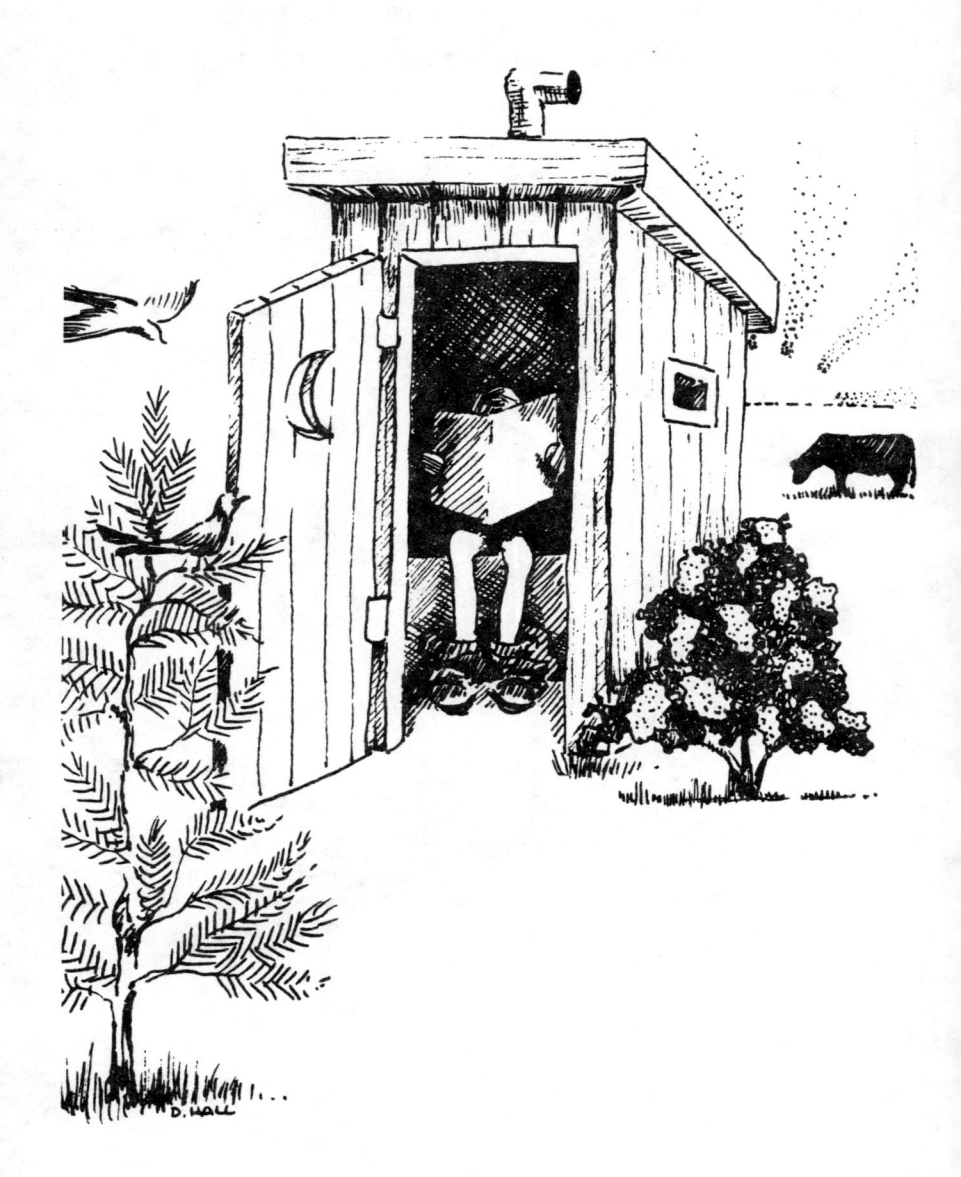
D. HALL

MEDITATION

Every mornin' about the break of day,
Nature calls and I make my way
To that little white house by the lilac bush.
I pull open the door and give it a push
So it stays wide open and I can feel the breeze
And watch the birds in the cedar trees.

Now I was sittin' there feelin' plum eternal,
Thumbin' through the <u>High Plains Journal</u>.
When I came to the meditation of the day
And the title read, "Take Time to Pray".
So I sat there and read it through
And it kinda seemed like the right thing to do.
So I said, "Thank you, Lord, that I'm alive and well,
Though I know sometimes it's hard to tell.
I'm always complainin' about the rye and the cheat
And never satisfied with the price of wheat.

And it seems every Sunday when church is to begin,
The cows get out and I have to put 'em back in.
I suppose it'd make a lot more sense
If I'd go out Saturday and fix the fence."

I pray for my daughter when she's low and blue,
And college is startin', will I get her through?
I pray for my wife when she's feelin' pain,
The fields are dry, we could use some rain.
I pray for the children that are hungry and ill
And I pray for the ones that the bullets kill.

"Well, I guess that's all, Lord, can't think of no more."
So I put down the lid and closed the door.
Well, I stood there for a moment, it was quiet as a mouse,
And I said, "Thank you, Lord, for my little outhouse."

OUTDOOR COMFORT

There's nothin' more relaxin'
Or as peaceful, don't you know,
As that house out by the lilacs
When you need a place to go.

With a magazine in your hand
And a gentle blowin' breeze,
It's almost tranquilizin'
As the birds play in the trees.

The redbirds are a singin'
And the squirrels are makin' racket
As my eyes become plumb fixed
On a large nest of yellow jacket.

They seem a little restless,
In fact they're quite uneasy.
The thought of stingin' yellow jackets
Makes my stomach queasy.

Should I finish and move slowly
Until I get clear out the door,
Or pull up my pants and run
While I pray that they don't score.

To my regret I chose the latter
And jumped up to start the race.
But, with my pants around my knees,
I fell flat upon my face.

Those yellow jackets were a buzzin';
I felt the stings on my behind.
As I ran like heck for safety,
It was matter over mind.

It took three days of soakin'
With bakin' soda on my bottom,
But I went back with gasoline
And made darn sure I got 'em.

Winter's not near as dangerous,
But it's not quite so fine.
When bare flesh touches hardwood,
It sends shivers up your spine.

Yet there's something said of winter,
When the snow is on the ground.
You may have to hurry faster,
But those yellow jackets aren't around.

We husbands don't always give enough credit to our wives for the things they do for us. We too often take them for granted. So I wrote this poem for my wife and all of you hard working wives out there. However, should we forget a birthday or anniversary, we might be in trouble.

FARM WIVES

Farm wives are special gals,
Most us guys agree.
I know mine has an extra task.
She has to live with me.

I don't know what I'd do
With no one to make the bed,
Or cook the meals that keep me goin'
And bake that homemade bread.

Sometimes she runs the tractor;
Gets parts when I'm broke down.
Helps doctor calves, mows the yard,
And hauls the wheat to town.

I know at least a hundred times
She's heard me yell and shout,
"When the chain gets tight just give it heck
Till it pulls the thing clear out!"

She's done a thousand loads of laundry
Of greasy jeans and mud,
Coveralls with branding smoke
And fresh manure and blood.

She's a whiz on the computer,
But I don't have time to learn.
You'll find me at the coffee shop
When I've got time to burn.

She teaches Sunday school, leads the choir,
Keeps this poet on the go;
Cans the garden, tends her flowers,
And still has time to sew.

Too many farmers are just like me
And take their wives for granted.
A night on the town is pay enough
When all the wheat is planted.

But wives need much more than that.
They need a hug along the way,
"I love ya...thanks for bein' here;
Good job you did today."

I FORGOT

I forgot my anniversary,
And now I'm really blue.
She forgot my supper
And my laundry, too.

She forgot to wash the dishes
And wouldn't speak to me.
Then she took my checkbook
On a real big shopping spree.

She forgot to let me sleep in bed
And I feel like a louse.
She tied my underwear in knots.
I'm in the old dog house.

I tried to say I'm sorry,
But all she does is pout.
She trashed my fishing poles
And threw my stuffed bass out.

When our anniversary rolls 'round next year,
I'll bet I don't forget.
She said she'd have the dog and me
Both neutered by the vet.

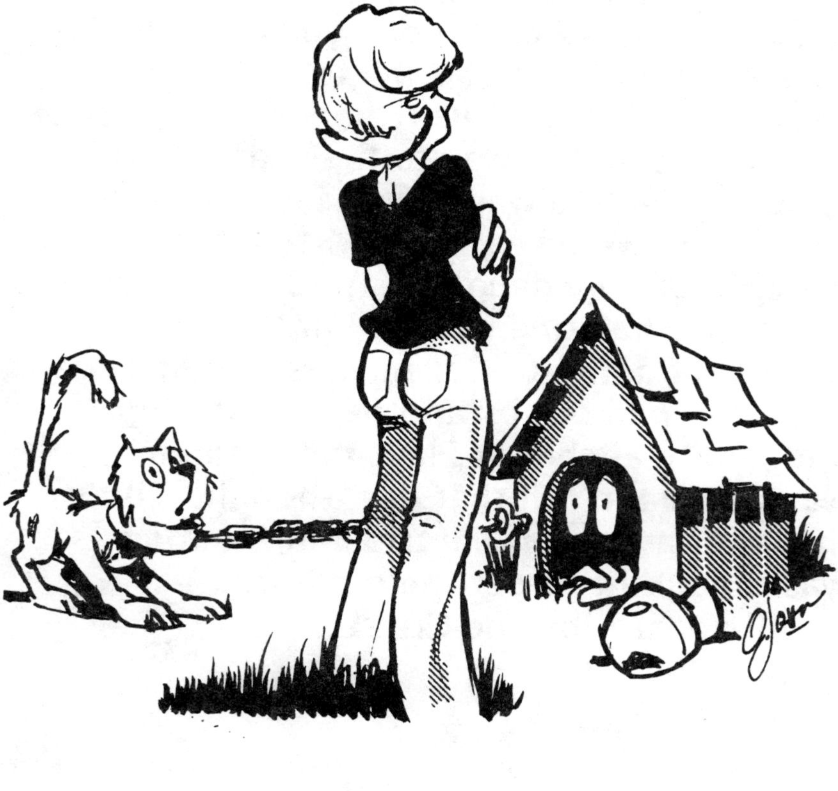

For our 25th wedding anniversary I decided to take my wife on a cruise and, since the third and fourth person could go for very little money, we took our 20-year-old daughter and her boyfriend (both in college). If you can imagine four of us in an 8-foot by 12-foot room with four bunk beds and a very small bathroom, you are starting to get the picture. The worst cold front of that winter followed us from New Orleans to Tampa and all the way to the Grand Cayman Islands. The sea was rough and many on board ship were sea sick. Fortunately we weren't, but my daughter and I both caught colds. We had one nice day in Mexico, but instead of going to Cozemel as planned, we were bumped out by another cruise ship and had to anchor at Playa del Carmen. It was warm and fun that day, though. This made for a memorable trip and the food was great, but forget the romance.

All aboard for The Cruise.

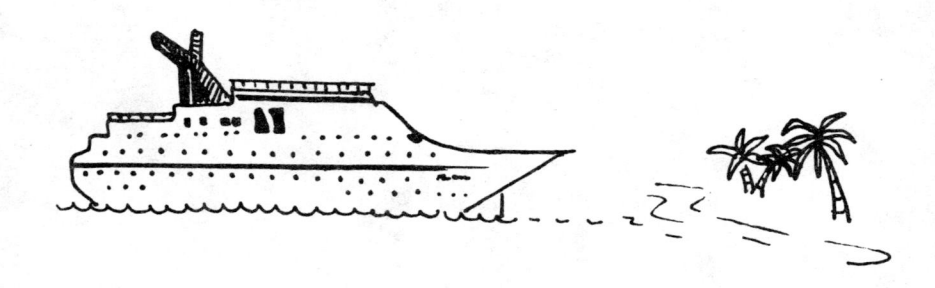

THE CRUISE

When the wheat was sowed.
And the work had slowed,
Thought we might have some fun.

Do a little sightseein',
Down in the Caribbean,
And check out the sand and sun.

We could take a cruise,
Cure the winter blues,
The food would all be free.

So I gave 'em a call
At the travel mall
And asked," What can you do for me?"

She said...
"It's a real neat ship,
Includes air fare and tip,
You sure won't find no junk.

The shows are great,
The food's first rate,
And you get an upper and lower bunk."

I said, "Ma'am...
It's our anniversary trip,
And our first cruise ship.
My wife, she might be frantic.

For I fear and I dread
That a two bunk bed
Might not be too romantic."

"Well, there's a room for four,
It's just next door,
The kids can cruise for free.

So, what the heck,
There's a baby-sitter on deck
So you can have your privacy."

I said, "Ma'am, these kids, you see,
That are cruisin' free,
I really should acknowledge.

My daughter dear
And her boyfriend here,
Well, they both go to college."

"It'll all work out,
I have no doubt.
Just let me see your card."

So I charged it all,
At the travel mall.
It wasn't all that hard.

But to get our share
Of the low air fare,
She said it'd be a pity,

If we didn't go
A few miles or so
And drive to Oklahoma City.

The day did arrive
For our three hour drive
To the airport at OKC.

I didn't mind the cold
Because I'd been told
How warm this trip would be.

The flight was okay,
Except for the one hour delay.
It made me a little nervous.

If we were late,
They wouldn't wait.
There wasn't water taxi service.

The fifteen minute trip
From airport to ship
Made me want to holler.

I had to cuss,
As we loaded the bus.
'Round trip was eighty dollar.

When we got to the pier,
We all did cheer.
It was just like we'd been told.

But as we boarded the ship
For our fantasy trip,
It seemed a tad bit cold.

When we opened the door
To our room for four,
We stood and stared a lot.

Like the woman said,
There were four bunk beds
And one small shower and pot.

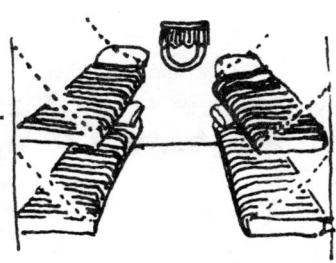

We sailed out that night,
To everyone's delight,
And sat down to our first night's dinner.

As I told the waiter,
Mandarin duck and baked 'tater,
I knew we'd get no thinner.

They brought everything,
It was fit for a king,
Until we could eat no more.

But as we walked on out,
I had no doubt,
There was movement in the floor.

We were rocked to sleep
On the ocean deep,
Pulled into Tampa in the morning.

Busch Gardens we'd see,
Felt half warm to me,
We really had no warning.

The rain came down,
We were all half drowned.
The wind began to blow.

We were wet and froze,
So we dried out in the shows
Till it was time to go.

We'd had quite a day,
As the ship pulled away.
Maybe tomorrow there'll be some sun.

We can lay by the pools
With the rest of the fools
And try to have some fun.

But when the sun did rise,
There were cloudy skies.
The sea was gettin' rough.

This wasn't too neat.
The waves were fifteen feet.
I'd about had enough.

The casino was fun,
But we had a dry run.
My luck it don't go far.

On the quarter slots
We missed all the pots,
But got a free drink at the bar.

The night time show
Rocked to and fro.
I don't know how they did it.

For I held on tight
To the pot that night.
I didn't know if I could hit it.

Grand Cayman came,
It was more of the same,
Cloudy and sixty degrees.

We only got to shop
On the half day stop
And watch the rollin' seas.

They had a talent show,
So I thought I'd go
Do a Sodbuster poem or two.

But I should have known,
These folks weren't farm grown,
And they didn't have a clue.

But my daughter sang.
It was the best darn thing.
She did a country song.

And of all the songs they did,
She was the only kid
That sang country all week long.

After a night at sea,
Glory be!
The coast of Mexico.

I can see the sun!
Let's have some fun.
A snorkelin' we can go.

Things will be swell
In Cozumel.
Should be more fun than farmin'.

But another Carnival ship
Screwed up the trip.
We had to anchor at Playa del Carmen.

We swam in the sea.
Was great to me.
My wife, she shopped a lot.

The sun shined all day
And it felt okay,
Even with the cold I'd caught.

But before you know,
It was time to go.
Our skin was gettin' red.

Back to New Orleans
And the Cajun queens,
As we all crawled in bed.

We awoke at the pier.
It was back home from here.
Our cruise was at an end.

We'd gone a long ways
In seven days.
2500 miles we'd been.

As we pulled in the yard,
We were all dead tired.
Yet we'd had a pretty good trip.

Some friends were made,
But I'm afraid
I wouldn't make it on a ship.

There's no tractor or truck;
No combine to get stuck;
The rooms are just too small.

There's no grain to scoop.
There's no cow poop,
And no outhouse most of all.

TEDDY

Sometimes we need a special friend,
One to really care.
Someone that's cute and furry
Like my favorite teddy bear.

I tell him all my problems
And he never makes a peep.
He's always there to watch me play
And by me when I sleep.

He never does complain,
Though I drag him by the mile.
I toss him, throw him, hug him,
And he always has a smile.

There are lots of friends I like.
I love my parents, too,
But they can't do everything
That a teddy bear can do.

He listens to my problems
And plays the games I like.
He helps me get to sleep at night
And rides upon my bike.

I probably will grow up someday
And travel here and there,
But I know that I will always love
My favorite teddy bear.

THE

SODBUSTER'S

WISDOM

LIFE'S WALK

When we begin our walk of life,
Before we ever talk,
We learn a lesson tried and true
To crawl before we walk.

Then we learn to play
And life is so much fun.
Our parents tell us every day
To walk before we run.

Then school begins
And we just have a ball.
The teachers make it very clear,
No running in the hall.

Don't track mud in the house.
Take your shoes off at the door.
Keep your feet off of the furniture
At least a thousand times or more.

Walk barefoot through the mud.
Feel it squish between your toes.
Walk a mile in someone else's shoes
To understand their woes.

We sometimes take the troubled path
And feel we cannot bear it.
Our friends may say it's all our fault.
If the shoe fits we must wear it.

But don't give up the race,
Though there be a thousand laps.
The Lord will help you pull yourself
Up by your bootstraps.

Don't walk a mile for a Camel
Or walk on the wild side.
Walk the straight and narrow road
For the One they crucified.

The roads we travel twist and turn.
Be wise the path you choose.
Remember if we walk by faith,
We can all fit in God's shoes.

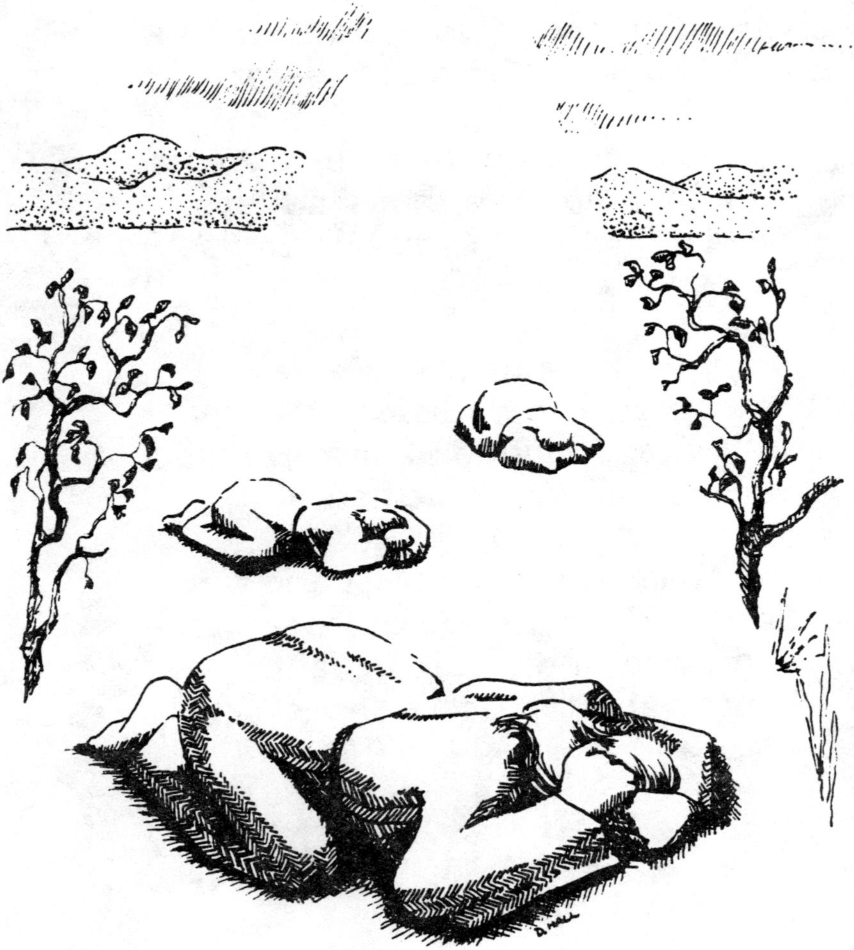

This is a poem taken from the Book of Acts about Stephen's death and Paul's conversion.

A CHANGED MAN

There was a group of righteous men,
Pharisees they say,
They searched out believers
That thought Jesus was the Way.

They arrested a faithful man
And vowed they would get even.
The Holy Spirit showed on his face.
That faithful man was Stephen.

They accused him of blasphemy
And told of how he lied.
But he called them stiff necked heathen
At whose hands Christ had died.

The Pharisees were angry
And dragged him from the city.
They laid their coats at the feet of Saul
And stoned Stephen without pity.

The stones came down at Stephen,
But before they did him in,
He said, "Lord, receive my spirit.
Do not charge them with this sin."

Saul became obsessed
With searching Christians out.
He dragged them from their houses.
His wrath it left no doubt.

Saul traveled to Damascus
To bring believers back,
Imprison them in Jerusalem
And put them on the rack.

But on the road a bright light flashed.
They fell upon the ground.
"Saul, why do you hate me so?"
The voice was all around.

Saul said, "Who speaks to me?
Is your aim to rob and loot?"
The voice said, "I am Jesus,
The one you persecute."

"Go wait inside the city.
My instructions you will find."
But, as Saul stood to leave,
He found that he was blind.

For three days Saul neither ate nor drank.
He prayed to God in grief.
The Lord told Ananias
To go give Saul relief.

Ananias went to Judas' house
And laid his hands on Saul.
He received the Holy Spirit
And they baptized him as Paul.

Paul taught the words of Jesus
To both Gentiles and Jews.
All Christian people owe the church
To his preaching The Good News.

The thoughts for this poem were taken from chapters 5, 6 and 7 of Matthew. It's the Sodbuster's interpretation of how Jesus' words apply to us today.

TIMELESS WORDS

It's 1997, Lord,
And I just want to know.
Those words that Matthew said you spoke,
Today are they still so?

The just and good you talked about,
I surely fit the bill.
I go to church on Sunday
And I pray for all the ill.

I'm sittin' here in church, Lord,
Bein' merciful and meek.
More humble than the others are;
I don't get up and speak.

My heart is pure as gold, you know.
I make peace when I try.
But I'm still mad at what's his name,
Although I don't remember why.

I've been persecuted, Lord;
I'm not treated very nice.
I told them how to run the church,
But they won't take my advice.

You say that I risk judgment
When I call names and curse my friends.
I'm supposed to say I'm sorry
And reconcile before day ends?

Lord, it's hard to be a light
And turn the other cheek;
Especially love your enemies,
Not criticize the weak.

I try to go the extra mile;
I shun lust and divorce.
But it's 1997 this year;
It's hard to stay the course.

I don't store up treasures, Lord;
Extravagant I'm not.
I need those shiny cars and things
To keep the image that I've got.

Do good deeds secretly;
Pray all alone, you say.
Don't be anxious for tomorrow;
Live life day by day.

Don't worry about the neighbor's speck
When you've got the log.
Beware of those false teachers
And don't give pearls to a hog.

I want to bear good fruit
And tell people about the Bible.
But I'm afraid to get involved;
I don't want to be held liable.

All religious men aren't godly;
Some are just good talk.
So do what the wise man did
And build on solid rock.

They're all hard things to live by, Lord,
Yet you've helped to ease my mind.
If I ask it will be given;
If I seek then I will find.

Yes, it's 1997, Lord,
And I guess I'd have to say.
Those words that Matthew said you spoke,
They're still quite true today.

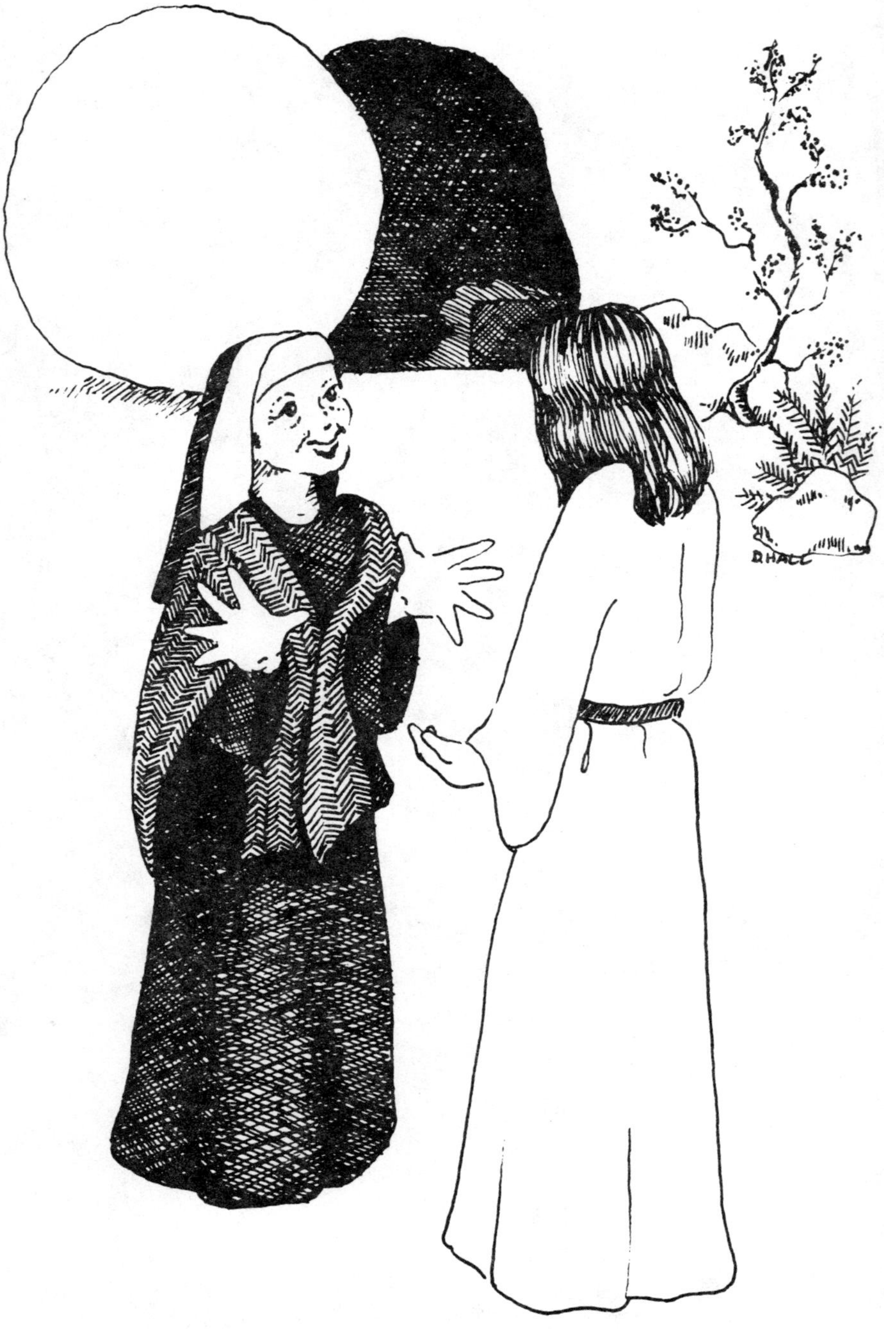
D HALL

MY SON

Two nights I've laid awake and cried,
You see, my Son was crucified.

I feel alone and so confused.
If one more miracle he would have used.

He'd saved himself for all to see
And be here now to comfort me.

This man, conceived in my own womb,
He now lays helpless in the tomb.

One last time I'll look at dawn.
The stones rolled back! The body's gone!

How could this be? What have they done?
Thieves have stolen my first born son!

The disciples! We must go!
I'm so afraid. They have to know.

This strange man who walks with me.
He sounds familiar. Who is He?

Then all at once I'm spirit filled!
My Son's with me, though He was killed.

The words should have been no surprise.
"Three days shall pass and He will rise."

Now I know the words were true.
His spirit lives in me and you.

THE SEASON

Christmas should be fun,
But for me it's kind of rough.
I don't much care for shopping lines,
Or all that junk and stuff.

Some say I'm old-fashioned,
Or just a scrooge, I guess.
But I think our society
Has become a great big mess.

Why do we buy those things?
Do we do it for our kids?
Why, I've seen them play with boxes,
Pots and pans and lids.

What have we become?
Our kids all say they're bored.
Do they know Christmas is
The birthday of our Lord?

Christmas time's for family
And sharing with the poor.
Not outdoing everyone
By buying more and more.

Homemade fudge and candy,
All kinds of fresh baked bread.
The taste of Mom's peanut brittle
Is locked securely in my head.

I like the simple, handmade things,
The ones made part by part.
You always know they're special
And they come straight from the heart.

So when Christmas rolls 'round this year,
Just use a little thought.
Go easy on the presents,
But try to love a lot.

SUCCESS

What kind of standard do we use?
Does the scale read more or less?
Can you tell by merely looking
How to measure one's success?

Can you tell it by the clothes we wear
Or from the shoes we buy?
What's our job description?
Do we wear a suit and tie?

Do we judge it by the cars we drive
Or houses that we own?
Does it require computers
And a cellular car phone?

Is it determined by our friends?
Are they politically correct?
Do our kids have all the best of things?
What goals do they select?

Or is success a state of mind,
Not judged by dumb or smart,
But by the way we've lived our lives,
The goodness of our heart.

Are we humble and unselfish?
Do we give without regret?
Do we teach our kids to help the poor
And work for what they get?

Do we instill confidence in them
And support them in the race?
Or do we demand they're number one,
No excuse for second place.

Success should mean happiness,
The love of work and life.
A Christian home of servitude
Unknown to greed and strife.

Most of us fall sadly short;
We fail to make the grade.
We're more concerned with status
And the money that we've made.

I'd like to think I've had success.
Life's treated me quite kind.
Yet I've always been concerned with self,
Letting others fall behind.

When the roll is read up yonder,
I pray I'll get the call.
Then I'll know my life has been
Successful after all.

ORDER FORM

To order additional copies of **_The Sodbuster's Wit and Wisdom,_** complete the information below.

Ship to: (please print)
Name_____
Address_____
City, State, Zip_____
Day phone_____

____copies of **_The Sodbuster's Wit & Wisdom_**
@$9.95 each $_____
Postage and handling @ $1.50 each $_____
Kansas residents add 4.9% tax $_____
Total amount enclosed $_____

Book I, **_The Sodbuster Poet, Poems by Danny Smith,_** plus two 30-minute cassette tapes are also available. Quantity discounts are offered. Contact the author for more information.

Make checks payable to Danny Smith

Send to: The Sodbuster Poet
1754 W. 130th Ave. N.
Milton, KS 67106
Phone - (316) 478-2496
e-mail - sodbusterpoet@juno.com

ORDER FORM

To order additional copies of **_The Sodbuster's Wit and Wisdom_**, complete the information below.

Ship to: (please print)
Name_____
Address_____
City, State, Zip_____
Day phone_____

_____copies of **_The Sodbuster's Wit & Wisdom_**
@$9.95 each $_____
Postage and handling @ $1.50 each $_____
Kansas residents add 4.9% tax $_____
Total amount enclosed $_____

Book I, **_The Sodbuster Poet, Poems by Danny Smith,_** plus two 30-minute cassette tapes are also available. Quantity discounts are offered. Contact the author for more information.

Make checks payable to Danny Smith

Send to: The Sodbuster Poet
1754 W. 130th Ave. N.
Milton, KS 67106
Phone - (316) 478-2496
e-mail - sodbusterpoet@juno.com